Editor
Eric Migliaccio

Managing Editor
Ina Massler Levin, M.A.

Editor-in-Chief
Sharon Coan, M.S. Ed.

Illustrator
Kevin Barnes

Cover Artist
Brenda DiAntonis

Art Coordinator
Kevin Barnes

Art Director
CJae Froshay

Imaging
James Edward Grace
Rosa C. See

Product Manager
Phil Garcia

Publishers
Rachelle Cracchiolo, M.S. Ed.
Mary Dupuy Smith, M.S. Ed.

BUILDING to SPELLING

Grades 1 & 2

Authors

Karen Piovarcsik and Susanne Schaeffer, M.A.

Teacher Created Materials, Inc.
6421 Industry Way
Westminster, CA 92683
www.teachercreated.com

ISBN-0-7439-3284-6

©2003 Teacher Created Materials, Inc.
Made in U.S.A.

Table of Contents

The Building Blocks to Spelling Program

Building Blocks to Spelling is a classroom and homework program designed to teach students the phonics rules for spelling, as well as to help first graders learn basic sight words. The program is divided into 32 weeks. Each week covers one or two phonics rules and between two to four sight words. The rules are written on each week's list of spelling words. Rules from previous weeks are reviewed on the subsequent lists so that parents and teachers can continue to reinforce the rules. One of the goals is to teach and reinforce the phonics rules rather than have students memorize the words. The phonics rules addressed in this program cover the following:

* short vowels
* long vowels
* consonant digraphs
* two- and three-letter blends
* r-controlled vowels

* vowel dipthongs (for example, *oi, oy, au, aw, ow,* and *ou*)
* consonant patterns (for example, *ph, kn, wr, dge, tch, ge, gi, ce,* and *ci*)
* word endings (for example, *–ed* and *–ing*)

The other goal is to make it clear to students that some words do not follow rules and must be memorized. Towards the end of the program, we have added spelling sentences that incorporate the spelling words of the week. Practicing these will help students learn basic punctuation, correct use of capitals, and correct spacing between words.

The spelling words are displayed in a flash-card format to make them easy to study. Each week's lesson has easy-to-use worksheets to help the students learn the rules and the sight words. The program also has hands-on activities for the teacher to use to help the students review the spelling and phonics lessons. A spelling test may be given after each week's lesson to assess the student's progress.

Language Arts Standards

Building Blocks to Spelling combines several language arts standards for grades 1–2. The program will help students progress from learning how to represent all the phonemes in simple words to representing words that have more advanced phonetic rules and unpredictable patterns of spelling. Students will also learn to segment words by their sounds and learn many phonics rules through step-by-step instruction. With continual practice, they will begin to learn conventionally correct spelling and they will be exposed to basic sight words that should be memorized. Below are the standards the program addresses:

➤ **Writing and Language Conventions (First Grade)**

Standard 1.8: Spell three- and four-letter short-vowel words and grade-level-appropriate sight words correctly.

Standard 1.5: Use a period, exclamation point, or question mark at the end of sentences.

Standard 1.6: Use knowledge of the basic rules of punctuation and capitalization when writing.

➤ **Writing and Language Conventions (Second Grade)**

Standard 1.7: Spell frequently used irregular words correctly (e.g., *was, were, says, said, who, what, why*).

Standard 1.8: Spell basic short-vowel, long-vowel, r-controlled, and consonant-blend patterns correctly.

How to Use the Program

You may want to wait to begin this program until the students know all the names of the letters of the alphabet and are familiar with the sounds of the consonants. The students should also have good phonemic awareness and be able to hear the beginning, middle, and ending sounds of words before you begin this program.

Below is a suggested weekly plan for using the program. You may want to spend more than one week on a particular list if it seems to be too difficult for the students. Send home the parent letter (page 12) explaining this spelling program if you choose to send spelling home for homework.

Day 1

---

1. First, you must work on **reading** the words. This is a precursor to spelling. Get out the spelling list. Introduce the sounds of all the consonants in the words, excluding the sight words. If the children do not know the sounds of these consonants, you will have to take the time to work on these consonant sounds.

2. Explain the phonics rule—which is usually what the sound of the vowel is—to the class. Have the students think of words that have the targeted sound. For example, ask, "Who can think of a word that has the short vowel **a** like in *lamb*?" Say various words and ask the students if the words have that sound or not.

3. Now, pick one of the words from the spelling list that follows the targeted rule. Put up one sound of the word at a time. As you put up each sound, have the students say the sound. Make sure they say the sound and not the name of the letter. Continue to build the word, sound by sound. When you have written the whole word, have the students go back and read the whole word. You can underline the sound you are working on. For example, if you are working on long /**a**/, you should underline the letters or letter that make this sound. If the word is **pail**, underline the **ai** and make sure to put these letters up as one sound.

pail

4. You can make this more fun by having the students use their hands to help them sound out and build the word. Have the students start by holding their hands together in front of them as if they had just finished clapping. As you put up each sound, have the students move their hands a little farther apart. Continue until all the sounds of the word are up. When the word is finished, have the students say the word and clap their hands at the same time. We call this "**Zap** it apart, and then **Clap** it."

5. As you write each word, have the students think of a sentence with that word in it. Make sure the students understand the meaning of all the words or know how to use the words in sentences. After all the words that follow the rules are up, review the words. You can have individual students come up, read a word, and then erase it. This can be called the "**Eraser** game."

How to Use the Program *(cont.)*

────────────── **Day 1** (cont.) ──────────────

6. Sight words should not be taught this way. Put up all of the letters of each sight word at one time. Use the word in a sentence. Work on memorizing each word. Some ideas from memorizing these words are as follows:

   • Make up a cheer and spell out all of the letters out loud in the word. For example, "*t-h-e* spells *the.*" Repeat several times. Clap or move body parts as you do it!
   • You can sing the letters as you spell the word.
   • You can go around the room and have every child spell the word so that they are hearing it over and over.
   • As each child leaves or enters the classroom, have that child spell one of the sight words.
   • Continue to review the sight words daily, using the teacher activities provided (or use your own).

────────────── **Day 2** ──────────────

1. Use one of the spelling worksheets to review the words, phonics rules, and sight words. This may be sent home as homework for the parents or completed in class.

2. Choose one of the teacher activities from the teacher activity pages (pages 10–11) to review the words and rules in class. A good activity for Day 2 is to sound out the words and have the children practice writing them on small white boards or chalkboards.

3. You should repeat Day 1's lesson using the same words and other words that follow the same rule.

────────────── **Day 3** ──────────────

1. Use a different spelling worksheet in class or choose to send it home as homework.

2. Choose another teacher activity to review the words and rules. A good activity for Day 3 is Spelling Bingo.

────────────── **Day 4** ──────────────

1. Choose another teacher activity to do in class. This may be a good day to have the students write sentences using the words.

2. Have the students take a practice spelling test at home or in class to help prepare them for the spelling test. Have parents—or you, the teacher—help students on words they spelled incorrectly. If the child does not seem to understand the phonics rule, continue to work on the rule at home and at school. Continue to repeat Day 1's building words lesson if the students still do not understand the phonics rule.

────────────── **Day 5** ──────────────

1. Choose a final teacher activity. Spelling Basketball is a good whole-group game.

2. Take the spelling test. In the beginning month or two of the school year, the teacher may sound out the spelling words for the students for the test.

3. You may want to use an incentive program to motivate students to do well on the tests.

Continue to use this weekly schedule with each new spelling list. Many of the lists have more than one rule. Make sure to continue to build, using all of the rules included in the targeted spelling words. Also, include other words that follow the rules, as the emphasis is on the phonics sounds.

Sequence of Skills

➤ Week 1
Introduce consonant sounds: **m**, **t**, **p**, and **h**. Introduce the sound of short vowel **/a/**. The letter **a** can make the sound **/a/** like in the word **lamb**.
Word list: map, mat, at, pat, ham, tap, am, hat
Sight words: to, I, the, is

➤ Week 2
Introduce consonant sounds: **s**, **d**, **c**, and **n**.
Word list: sat, sad, mad, can, cat, cap, tan, an
Sight words: and, he, me, be

➤ Week 3
Introduce the short vowel **i**. The letter **i** can make the sound **/i/** like in the word **pig**.
Word list: and, hand, sand, it, sit, hip, did, pin
Sight words: the, he, of, as

➤ Week 4
Introduce consonant sounds: **f**, **g**, **b**. Review short vowel sounds **/a/** and **/i/**.
Word list: fat, fan, fin, pig, big, dig, fast, if
Sight words: see, go, or, we

➤ Week 5
Introduce consonant sounds: **r** and **x**. Introduce the short vowel **o**. The letter **o** can make the sound **/o/** like in the word **frog**.
Word list: hot, stop, frog, top, box, fox, fix, six
Sight words: says, have, do, by

➤ Week 6
Introduce the sound **/ar/**. The letters **ar** together make the sound **/ar/** like in the word **arm**.
Word list: car, bar, barn, far, star, arm, farm, hard
Sight words: are, my, you, was

➤ Week 7
Introduce the consonant **z**. Introduce the short vowel sound of **/u/**. The letter **u** can make the sound **/u/** like in the word **bug**.
Word list: up, cup, fun, run, bug, rug, but, zip
Sight words: me, do, with, this

➤ Week 8
Introduce consonants: **l**, **k**, **w**, **y**. Introduce short vowel **e**. The letter **e** can make the sound **/e/** like in the word **hen**. Introduce this rule: Use the letters **ck** after a short vowel to make the **/k/** sound.
Word list: let, wet, yet, help, lock, clock, duck, deck
Sight words: for, said, they, have

Sequence of Skills *(cont.)*

➣ **Week 9**

Introduce the consonant digraphs **sh** and **th**. The letters **sh** can make the sound **/sh/** like in the word **shark**. The letters **th** can make the sound **/th/** like in the word **thumb**.
Word list: this, that, thin, with, shark, shop, fish, wish
Sight words: what, when, for, are

➣ **Week 10**

Introduce the consonant digraph **ch**. The letters **ch** can make the sound **/ch/** like in the word **chipmunk**.
Word list: chin, chip, chick, lunch, inch, much, shell, math
Sight words: she, her, his, from

➣ **Week 11**

Introduce the concept of long vowels. A long vowel sound is the same as the name of that vowel. Introduce long vowel **a** with "magic **e**." An **e** at the end of a word can make a vowel say its name. We call it the "magic **e**." A magic **e** can jump back only one letter in a word to make the vowel long.
Word list: ate, gate, cake, rake, made, whale, shape, tape
Sight words: were, you, one, what

➣ **Week 12**

Introduce the long vowel **i** and the long vowel **o** with magic **e** rule. When there is an **e** at the end of a word, it will make the first vowel say its name. Introduce the rule that the consonant **s** can sometimes make the sound **/z/** like in **zipper** when it is between two vowels.
Word list: ride, hide, nice, mice, nose, rose, drove, vote
Sight words: no, like, yes, all

➣ **Week 13**

Introduce the long vowels **u** and **e** with magic **e**. Introduce the rule that when there are two vowels together, the first vowel does the talking and the second vowel does the walking. In other words, the first vowel says its name. Show that the letters **ee** make the long vowel sound of **/e/**. The consonant **g** can sometimes make the sound **/j/** when it is followed by an **e** or **i**.
Word list: use, fuse, cute, huge, sheep, street, meet, green
Sight words: be, we, what, when

➣ **Week 14**

Introduce that the two vowels **ea** can make the long vowel **/e/** sound. Introduce the consonants **qu** and consonant blends **scr**, **squ**, and **dr**. Spelling sentences will now be added to the program. The sentence will incorporate the spelling words. The children should have been introduced to using a capital letter at the beginning of a sentence and a period at the end of a declarative (telling) sentence. Later, the correct use of the question mark and the exclamation point may be introduced. Capitalization in proper names should also be introduced. Correct spacing between words should also be emphasized.
Word list: eat, meat, each, scream, squeal, dream, quick, quit
Sight words: from, these, you, your

Sequence of Skills *(cont.)*

➤ **Week 15**

Introduce rule that a **y** at the end of the word can make the long vowel sound of **/e/**. Introduce that vowels **ai** make the long vowel sound of **/a/**. The letters **ay** make the long vowel sound of **/a/**.

Word list: lady, baby, pony, rain, mail, pail, play, say

Sight words: once, come, was, with

➤ **Week 16**

The letters **igh** make the long vowel **/i/** sound; the letter **y** can make the sound **/i/** at the end of a word.

Word list: right, night, sight, high, try, cry, dry, fly, why

Sight words: why, they, this, by

➤ **Week 17**

The letters **ow**, **oe**, and **oa** and the letter **o** can make the long vowel **/o/** sound.

Word list: snowman, yellow, grow, throw, boat, goat, float, cold, gold, toe

Sight words: was, saw

➤ **Week 18**

The letters **ew** and **ue** can make the long **/u/** sound; the letters **ow** can make the sound **/ow/** like in **cow**.

Word list: few, rescue, how, now, brown, cow, flower, downtown, shower

Sight words: which, were, when

➤ **Week 19**

Introduce that **ou** can make the sound like in **cow**; **au** and **aw** can make the sound like in **hawk**.

Word list: shout, house, mouse, about, saw, hawk, August, because, draw, paw

Sight words: who, were

➤ **Week 20**

Introduce the rule that the letters **oo**, **ew**, and **ue** can make a **/oo/** sound like in the word **moon**.

Word list: food, spoon, cool, moonlight, glue, blue, true, rule, grew, new

Sight words: with, have

➤ **Week 21**

Introduce that **oo** can make a sound like in **book**. Introduce that a **k** before an **n** is silent, as in **knee**.

Word list: look, book, cookie, good, knee, know, took, stood, knock

Sight words: put, there, where

➤ **Week 22**

Introduce the rule that the letters **oy** and **oi** can make a sound like in the word **toy**.

Word list: boy, enjoy, toy, coin, join, coil, spoil

Sight words: could, would, should, are, my

➤ **Week 23**

Introduce that **ph** can make the sound **f** like in **fun**. In words that start with **wr**, the **w** is silent.

Word list: wrong, write, wrap, wrinkle, photo, phone, graph, elephant, three, just

Sight words: friend, all

Sequence of Skills *(cont.)*

➤ Week 24
The letters **ed** can be added to make a word past tense; the letters **er** make the sound **/er/**, as in **her**.
Word list: asked, pulled, washed, planted, started, thunder, powder, carpenter, teacher, baker
Sight words: our, here

➤ Week 25
Introduce that the letters **er**, **ir**, and **ur** can make the sound **/ir/** as in **bird**.
Word list: church, burst, hurt, turn, bird, first, third, birthday
Sight words: little, thank, why, they

➤ Week 26
Introduce the rule that the letters **dge** are used after a short vowel to make the sound **/j/** like in **jump**.
Introduce the consonant blends **shr**, **scr**, **thr**, **spl**, **str**, and **squ**.
Word list: bridge, fudge, pledge, hedge, badge, judge, shred, scrape, throw, splash, squeak, strong

➤ Week 27
Introduce the rule that the letter **i** can make the long **/i/** sound.
Word list: find, kind, mind, behind, climb
Sight words: after, how, again, where, there, when, water

➤ Week 28
Introduce the rule that the letters **alk** represent a spelling pattern that makes the sound like in the word
walk. Introduce that the letters **all** represent a spelling pattern that makes the sound like in **call**.
Word list: walk, talk, chalk, fall, mall, smaller, all, call, tall, September, October
Sight words: does

➤ Week 29
Introduce that **ing** make the sound like in **king**. The letters **ly** make the sound like in **slowly**.
Word list: king, thing, running, jumping, flying, shouting, slowly, quickly
Sight words: was, saw, when, your

➤ Week 30
Review that **g** followed by **e** or **i** can sound like **/j/** in **jump**; **g** followed by an **n** is silent, as in **gnat**.
Word list: gnaw, gnash, gem, large, gentle, cage, giant, second
Sight words: want, when, there, their

➤ Week 31
Introduce that **y** at the end of a word can change to **i** when adding an ending on the end of the word.
Word list: happy, happier, happiest, funny, funnier, funniest, city, cities, baby, babies
Sight word: your, our

➤ Week 32
Introduce the rule that the letters **le** at the end of a word can make the sound **/l/** like in **table**.
Word list: table, candle, fable, fiddle
Sight words: one, two, four, eight, give, some, very, lived

Teacher Activities

Use these activities in class or at home to help learn the rules and the spelling words.

◊◊◊Spelling Basketball◊◊◊

Divide the class into two teams. Choose one person from each team to come up to the board. Give each child a different spelling word to write on the board. If the student gets it right, his/her team earns a point. Both students can earn points. The students also earn a chance to make a basket. Set up a bucket and place a piece of tape about seven feet away. The child stands on the tape and tries to shoot a basketball into the bucket. A bonus point is earned if the basket is made. Review the spelling words with the whole class before calling up the next two contestants.

◊◊◊Spelling Bingo◊◊◊

Create and distribute Spelling Bingo boards. (Boards should consist of a grid with 12 spaces; one of the spaces should be marked "Free Space." Students can fold pieces of blank paper to create these grids.) Say a spelling word and have the children write it anywhere on their boards. Review the word on the board or make sure the children are spelling it correctly. Continue until all the spaces on everyone's boards are completed. Pass out markers to cover up the words. Put the words on flash cards and place in a bag. Call out the words or have a student call them out. The students cover the words on their boards as they are called out. The first student who has words covered up in a vertical, horizontal, or diagonal row calls out "Bingo!"

◊◊◊Spelling Concentration◊◊◊

Make two sets of flash cards for the spelling list that is being worked on by the students. Work with a small group of students. Place all the cards facedown on the table. The child turns over a word and tries to find its match. The student with the most matches wins the game. If the word the child chose has a phonics rule, have the child tell the rule after he or she makes the match. If he or she doesn't know the rule, see if another student can tell him or her the rule; if not, review the rule with all the students.

◊◊◊Around the World Reading/Spelling Game◊◊◊

Teacher needs to make a set of flash cards for the spelling list used. One child is chosen to start the game. He/she stands behind another seated child. The teacher holds up the word for both children to see. The first child to read the word wins and gets to stand behind the next seated child. If the student who is standing does not win, he or she sits in the chair vacated by the winning student. The idea of the game is to get all around the classroom. This will help children read the words as well as spell them.

◊◊◊Flash Card Games◊◊◊

Give each child note cards. (You may also give them each a piece of paper. Have them fold this piece of paper into eight squares and then cut it up into the eight squares.) Have the children write on the flash cards the words that they think are the most difficult. After they have finished, put the children into pairs. Have each pair practice spelling the words. One child holds up his or her card and reads the word. The other child spells it. If the child spells it correctly, the card is put on the table. If the child spells it incorrectly, the card is put back into the pile. The children continue until all the cards are on the table.

Teacher Activities *(cont.)*

◇◇◇Practice Words on White Boards◇◇◇

Give each child a small white board and dry-erase marker. (You can also use chalkboards.) Have a child hold up his or her board so that the others cannot see it. You or a parent should say a spelling word. Then say the phonics rule that applies to that word. Have the children spell the word on their boards. When everyone is done, the children should put their boards down so you can see if they have spelled the word correctly. If any child spelled it wrong, review the word together and have the children write it one more time. Keep working until all the words have been used.

◇◇◇Practice Typing Words on Computer◇◇◇

If the students have access to computers, give each child a spelling list and have them practice typing each word one time on the computer. If possible, print out the finished product.

◇◇◇Go Fish with Spelling Words◇◇◇

Make up four sets of flash cards using the spelling words. Work with children in a small group. Pass out five cards to the children. Have the children hold up their cards so that no one can see them. Put the rest of the cards facedown in a pile. Each child has a turn. The first player gets to ask one other player if he has one of the same words in his hand. If the other player has the word, the child can put the pair facedown. Then, the child has to spell the word correctly. If the child cannot spell it correctly, he has to give the word back and the next child has a turn. If the child spells it correctly, he gets another turn. If the other player does not have the word in his hand, he says "Go fish!" and the other child takes a card from the deck. The group keeps playing until one child has all his cards down on the table. The child with the most cards wins the game.

◇◇◇Spelling Rule Contest◇◇◇

Give each child or pair of children a piece of paper. Pick one of the spelling rules. For example, a **y** at the end of a word can make the sound **/e/** like in **baby**. Write one word on the board to give them an example. Now tell them they will have five minutes to think of as many words that have that rule and write them on the paper. Say, "On your mark, get set, spell!" At the end of five minutes, collect the papers. The child with the most correctly spelled words wins a prize. Write his or her list on the board as a reward.

◇◇◇Make Up Sentences Using Spelling Words◇◇◇

Write the spelling words on the board or pass out a list to each child. Hand out paper and tell them to try to write sentences using the spelling words. Show them how they can use two or more words in one sentence. When they are finished, collect the papers and correct them. Pass them back out and have the students each pick one or more sentences to illustrate and then read to a friend.

Parent Letter

Dear Parents,

We will start our spelling program this week. Each Monday, I will send home a list of words with a matching rule. For example, in the first list we are focusing on the short /**a**/ sound. Work with your child on the rule. It should then be easy for your child to sound out the words.

There will be a few words on each list that are labeled as "sight words." These must be memorized through practice. You may need to spend more time on these words. Worksheets will come home as part of your child's homework to reinforce these words.

On Thursday, give your child a practice spelling test. Work on any words that he or she misses. If your child has not mastered the phonics rule, continue to practice.

On Friday, we will take a spelling test. For the first few weeks, I will be sounding out each word.

Your child will need the following materials to use at home:

- ❏ glue or tape
- ❏ scissors
- ❏ paper
- ❏ pencils
- ❏ crayons

Sincerely,

_____

Spelling Test

Name _____ Date _____

1.

2.

3.

4.

5.

6.

7.

8.

9.

10.

11.

12.

Spelling Sentence

Handwriting: Excellent   Good   Keep Practicing

Name: _____

Spelling Week 1

☆ **Week 1 Rule:** Short **a** says /a/ like in **lamb**.

map	**mat**	**at**	**pat**

am	**hat**	**ham**	**tap**

I	**to**	**is**	**the**
sight word	sight word	sight word	sight word

Sight words do not necessarily follow rules.

14

Name: _____

Spelling Fun

at	pat	am	hat	ham	to	map	tap

1. On the back of this paper, write each word one time.

2. Write three words from the list that rhyme with **cat**.

_____

- -

_____

- -

_____

- -

3. Write two words from the list that rhyme with **jam**.

_____

- -

_____

- -

4. Which two words from the list start with **t**?

_____   _____

-        -

_____   _____

5. Practice reading and spelling your words to a parent.

Name: _____

Unscramble the Sentence

Cut and paste the words onto the lines in the correct order to make a sentence. Use the capital and period as a clue. Draw a picture of your sentence.

ham.	The	hat	on	is	the

Name: _____

Word Search

Find and circle these spelling words.

map	at	am	ham	I	is
mat	pat	hat	tap	to	the

All words read horizontally and left to right. There may be other words in the puzzle that are not spelling words.

```
m  a  p  a  b  c  l  m  a  a  t  y  o  j  t

z  a  c  a  t  a  p  a  t  m  a  p  o  p  w

m  a  t  b  c  d  e  f  h  a  t  s  a  r  e

t  a  t  y  t  a  p  b  y  a  m  a  m  a  l

g  j  a  t  l  o  g  h  a  m  x  y  z  s  q

o  n  t  a  p  x  y  t  o  m  k  w  e  r  t

s  u  s  a  n  n  e  i  s  p  o  j  k  l  k

k  a  r  e  n  t  h  e  I  n  t  t  e  p  p
```

Name: _____

Spelling Week 2

☆ **Week 2 Rule:** Short **a** says **/a/** like in **lamb**.

sat	sad	mad	can

cat	cap	tan	an

and	he	be	me
sight word	sight word	sight word	sight word

Sight words do not necessarily follow rules.

Name: _____

Word Search

Find and circle these spelling words.

sat	mad	cat	tan	and	be
sad	can	cap	an	he	me

All words read horizontally and left to right. There may be other words in the puzzle that are not spelling words.

m	s	a	t	b	c	c	a	t	a	t	y	o	j	o
z	a	a	n	d	a	p	a	t	m	a	p	o	p	y
m	a	t	b	c	d	e	s	a	d	t	s	a	r	t
t	a	t	c	a	p	p	b	y	a	m	a	m	a	l
g	h	a	t	l	o	g	h	e	x	x	y	z	s	q
o	m	a	d	p	x	y	t	a	n	k	w	e	r	t
s	b	e	a	n	m	e	i	s	p	o	j	c	a	n
a	n	r	e	n	t	h	e	l	n	t	t	e	p	p

On the back of this page, draw a picture of this sentence.

I am mad at the tan cat.

Name: _____

Word Fun

sat	mad	cat	tap	and	me
sad	can	cap	an	he	be

1. Write each word one time each on the back of this paper.

2. Write a rhyming word from the list for each word below:

pan

bat

map

3. Unscramble the letters to make words from your list.

tsa _____

eb _____

sda _____

Name: _____

Unscramble the Sentence

Cut and paste the words onto the lines in the correct order to make a sentence.
Use the capital and period as clues. Draw a picture of your sentence.

cat.	He	sat	sad	on	the

Name: _____

Spelling Week 3

☆ **Week 3 Rules:** Short **a** says **/a/** like in **lamb**.

Short **i** says **/i/** like in **pig**.

and	**hand**	**sand**	**it**

sit	**hip**	**did**	**pin**

the	**he**	**of**	**as**
sight word	sight word	sight word	sight word

Sight words do not necessarily follow rules.

Name: _____

Sort the Vowels

Write the words under the word with the same short vowel sound.

and	sand	hip	pin
hand	sit	did	as

cat

_____

- - - - - - - - - - - - - - - - - - - -

_____

- - - - - - - - - - - - - - - - - - - -

_____

- - - - - - - - - - - - - - - - - - - -

_____

- - - - - - - - - - - - - - - - - - - -

_____

pig

_____

- - - - - - - - - - - - - - - - - - - -

_____

- - - - - - - - - - - - - - - - - - - -

_____

- - - - - - - - - - - - - - - - - - - -

_____

- - - - - - - - - - - - - - - - - - - -

_____

Name: _____

Word Search

Find and circle these spelling words.

and	sand	sit	hip	pin	he
hand	it	as	did	the	of

All words read horizontally and left to right. There may be other words in the puzzle that are not spelling words.

```
a  n  d  t  b  c  c  a  t  a  t  y  o  j  o

z  a  a  n  d  h  a  n  d  m  a  p  o  p  y

m  a  t  s  a  n  d  s  a  d  t  s  a  r  t

t  a  t  c  s  i  t  u  b  y  a  i  t  m  a

g  h  a  s  l  o  g  h  e  x  x  y  z  s  q

o  m  h  i  p  x  y  t  d  i  d  w  e  r  t

s  p  i  n  m  e  i  s  p  h  e  c  a  n  v

a  n  r  e  n  t  h  e  b  o  f  t  e  p  p
```

On the back of this page, draw a picture of this sentence.

I can sit in the sand.

24

Name: _____

Unscramble the Sentence

Cut and paste the words onto the lines in the correct order to make a sentence. Use the capital and period as a clue. Draw a picture of your sentence.

sit	He	can	sand.	in	the

Name: _____

Spelling Week 4

☆ **Week 4 Rules:** Short **a** says /a/ like in **lamb**.

Short **i** says /i/ like in **pig**.

fat	fan	fin	pig

big	dig	fast	if

see	go	or	we
sight word	sight word	sight word	sight word

Sight words do not necessarily follow rules.

Name: _____

Unscramble the Sentence

Cut and paste the words onto the line in the correct order to make a sentence. Use the capital and period as clues. Draw a picture of your sentence.

big	The	fat	pig	dig	can	fast.

Name: _____

Sort the Vowels

fat	fin	big	fast	see	or
fan	pig	dig	if	go	we

1. Which words have the short /i/ sound?

_____

- - - - - - - - - - - - - - - - - - - -

_____

_____

- - - - - - - - - - - - - - - - - - - -

_____

_____

- - - - - - - - - - - - - - - - - - - -

_____

_____

- - - - - - - - - - - - - - - - - - - -

_____

2. Which words have the short /a/ sound?

_____

- - - - - - - - - - - - - - - - - - - -

_____

- - - - - - - - - - - - - - - - - - - -

_____

- - - - - - - - - - - - - - - - - - - -

_____

Name: _____

Fill in the Missing Word

fat	fin	big	fast	see	or
fan	pig	dig	if	go	we

Fill in the missing word in each sentence.

1. The dog can _____ .

2. The fish has a _____ .

3. The _____ sits in the mud.

4. The hippo is _____ and _____ .

5. I _____ a big cat.

Name: _____

Spelling Week 5

☆ **Week 5 Rule:** Short **o** says /o/ like in **frog**.

Rules We've Learned

- Short **a** says /a/ like in **lamb**.
- Short **i** says /i/ like in **pig**.

hot	**stop**	**frog**	**top**

box	**fox**	**fix**	**six**

says	**have**	**do**	**by**
sight word	sight word	sight word	sight word

Sight words do not necessarily follow rules.

Name: _____

Word Search

Find and circle the spelling words. All words read horizontally and left to right. There may be words other than spelling words in the puzzle.

h	o	t	x	y	z	d	f	g	z	a	t
s	y	z	m	a	t	v	s	t	o	p	a
t	r	m	f	r	o	g	v	q	t	u	s
o	r	t	o	p	a	x	l	o	p	h	a
d	o	m	t	f	o	x	m	c	s	i	z
t	c	s	a	y	s	x	c	s	t	o	p
a	h	a	v	e	i	l	k	m	f	i	x
w	b	o	x	q	r	e	t	y	o	x	c
e	c	s	i	x	m	s	a	y	s	b	y

Spelling Words

hot

stop

frog

top

box

fox

fix

six

says

have

do

by

Draw a picture of the sentence in the box.

The frog is on top of the box.

Name: _____

Fill in the Missing Word

hot	frog	box	fix	says	do
stop	top	fox	six	have	by

Fill in the missing word in each sentence.

1. The cab will _____ .

2. I can kiss a green _____ .

3. I am _____ .

4. I am on _____ of the hill.

5. The cat is in the _____ .

6. I _____ six dogs.

Name: _____

Sort the Vowels

Write the words under the word with the same short vowel sound.

stop	box	fox	says
frog	fix	six	have

clock

_____

- - - - - - - - - - - - - - -

_____

_____

- - - - - - - - - - - - - - -

_____

_____

- - - - - - - - - - - - - - -

_____

zip

_____

- - - - - - - - - - - - - - -

_____

_____

- - - - - - - - - - - - - - -

_____

_____

- - - - - - - - - - - - - - -

_____

Name: _____

Spelling Week 6

☆ **Week 6 Rule:** The letters **ar** say **/ar/** like in **arm**.

Rules We've Learned
- Short **a** says **/a/** like in **lamb**.
- Short **i** says **/i/** like in **pig**.
- Short **o** says **/o/** like in **frog**.

car	**bar**	**barn**	**far**

star	**arm**	**farm**	**hard**

are	**my**	**you**	**was**
sight word	sight word	sight word	sight word

Sight words do not necessarily follow rules.

34

Name: _____

Spelling Art

Draw a picture of each word. Copy the word neatly.

car	**barn**	**star**
arm	**farm**	**you**

Name: _____

Unscramble the Sentence

Cut and paste the words onto the lines in the correct order to make a sentence. Use the capital and period as clues. Draw a picture of your sentence.

you	Are	too	far	the	from	star?

Name: _____

Sort the Sounds

car	barn	star	farm	are	you
bar	far	arm	hard	my	was

1. Which words have the /**ar**/ sound like in **arm**?

_____   _____

_____   _____

_____   _____

_____

_____

_____

_____

2. Which words do not have the /**ar**/ sound in them?

_____   _____

_____

Name: _____

Spelling Week 7

☆ **Week 7 Rule:** Short **u** says **/u/** like in **bug**.

Rules We've Learned

- The letters **ar** say **/ar/** like in **arm**.
- Short **a** says **/a/** like in **lamb**.
- Short **i** says **/i/** like in **pig**.
- Short **o** says **/o/** like in **frog**.

up	cup	fun	run

bug	rug	but	zip

me	do	with	this
sight word	sight word	sight word	sight word

Sight words do not necessarily follow rules.

Name: _____

Spelling Art

Draw a picture of each word. Copy the word neatly.

cup	bug	up

zip	rug	me

Name: _____

Rhyming Fun

1. Draw a line to match the rhyming words.

up	**fun**
rug	**cup**
run	**bug**

2. Trace each word. Then choose a rhyming word from the box and write it next to each word.

lip	**be**

_____

me _____

_____

zip _____

Name: _____

Fill in the Missing Word

up	fun	bug	but	me	with
cup	run	rug	zip	do	this

Fill in the missing word in each sentence.

1. Will you go with _____ ?

2. It is fun to _____ fast.

3. I can _____ it!

4. Can you go _____ me?

5. Is _____ your cat?

6. The _____ sat on the rug.

Name: _____

Spelling Week 8

☆ **Week 8 Rules:** Short **e** says **/e/** like in **hen**.

Always use the letters **ck** after a short vowel to make the **/k/** sound.

Rules We've Learned

- Short **u** says **/u/** like in **bug**.
- The letters **ar** say **/ar/** like in **arm**.

- Short **a** says **/a/** like in **lamb**.
- Short **i** says **/i/** like in **pig**.
- Short **o** says **/o/** like in **frog**.

let	wet	yet	help
lock	clock	duck	deck
for	said	they	have
sight word	sight word	sight word	sight word

Sight words do not necessarily follow rules.

42

Name: _____

Word Search

Find and circle the spelling words. All words read horizontally and left to right. There may be words other than spelling words in the puzzle.

m	l	e	t	c	l	m	w	e	t	z	a
t	x	y	z	y	e	t	v	w	s	a	i
h	a	v	e	l	o	p	h	e	l	p	l
m	x	l	o	c	k	x	c	v	d	o	c
d	f	r	d	u	c	k	l	x	f	o	r
f	g	j	i	d	e	c	k	a	p	e	f
o	r	q	u	e	s	t	m	s	a	i	d
c	l	o	c	k	t	y	t	h	e	y	m

Spelling Words

let

wet

yet

help

lock

clock

duck

deck

for

said

they

have

Draw a picture of the sentence in the box.

The wet duck said, "Help!"

Name: _____

Spelling Fun

let	yet	lock	duck	for	they
wet	help	clock	deck	said	have

1. On the back of this paper, write each word one time.

2. Write three words that rhyme with **met**.

_____ _____ _____

3. Write two words that rhyme with **sock**.

_____ _____

4. Which two words start with **d**?

_____ _____

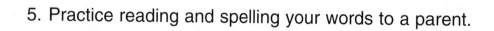

5. Practice reading and spelling your words to a parent.

Name: _____

Unscramble the Sentence

Cut and paste the words onto the lines in the correct order to make a sentence. Use the capital and period as clues. Draw a picture of your sentence.

have	They	a	duck.	wet

Name: _____

Spelling Week 9

☆ **Week 9 Rules:**   The letters **th** say **/th/** like in **thumb**.

The letters **sh** say **/sh/** like in **shark**.

Rules We've Learned

- Short **e** says **/e/** like in **hen**.
- Always use the letters **ck** after a short vowel to make the **/k/** sound.
- The letters **ar** say **/ar/** like in **arm**.
- Short **a** says **/a/** like in **lamb**.
- Short **i** says **/i/** like in **pig**.
- Short **o** says **/o/** like in **frog**.

this	that	thin	with
shark	**shop**	**fish**	**wish**
what	**when**	**for**	**are**
sight word	sight word	sight word	sight word

Sight words do not necessarily follow rules.

Name: _____

Riddle Fun

Answer the riddle. Write the correct word on the line.

thin	that	shark	shop	fish	wish

1. I'm not fat. I'm _____ .

2. I like to make a _____ upon a star.

3. Fat, cat, mat, and _____ all rhyme.

4. I rhyme with dish. I'm a _____ .

5. You don't want to swim with me. I'm a _____ .

6. My mom loves to _____ .

Name: _____

Unscramble the Sentence

Cut and paste the words onto the lines in the correct order to make a sentence. Use the capital and period as a clue. Draw a picture of your sentence.

is	What	that	for?	thin	fish

Name: _____

Sort the Sounds

this	thin	shark	fish	what	for
that	with	shop	wish	when	are

1. Which words have the **/th/** sound like in **thumb**?

_____   _____

_____   _____

_____   _____

_____   _____

2. Which words have the **/sh/** sound like in **ship**?

_____   _____

_____   _____

_____   _____

_____   _____

3. Which words have the **/wh/** sound like in **whale**?

_____

_____

_____

_____

4. Which word rhymes with **car**?

_____

_____

Name: _____

Spelling Week 10

☆ **Week 10 Rule:** The letters **ch** say **/ch/** like in **chipmunk**.

Rules We've Learned
- The letters **th** say **/th/** like in **thumb**.
- The letters **sh** say **/sh/** like in **shark**.
- Short **e** says **/e/** like in **hen**.
- Always use the letters **ck** after a short vowel to make the **/k/** sound.
- Short **u** says **/u/** like in **bug**.
- Short **a** says **/a/** like in **lamb**.
- Short **i** says **/i/** like in **pig**.

chin	chip	chick	lunch
inch	much	shell	math
she	her	his	from
sight word	sight word	sight word	sight word

Sight words do not necessarily follow rules.

Name: _____

Match the Picture

Name the picture. Circle the word for the picture. Then write the word on the line.

chin
thin
win

_____

much
lunch
inch

_____

chick
chin
ship

_____

with
math
what

_____

fish
fins
shell

_____

Name: _____

Unscramble the Sentence

Cut and paste the words onto the lines in the correct order to make a sentence. Use the capital and period as clues. Draw a picture of your sentence.

chick	is	shell.	The	still	her	in

Name: _____

Spelling Fun

chin	chick	inch	shell	she	his
chip	lunch	much	math	her	from

1. On the back of this paper, write each word one time.

2. Write three words that start with **ch.**

_____   _____
-    -
_____   _____
_____
- - - - - - - - - - - - - - - - - - - -
_____

3. Write two words that start with **sh.**

_____   _____
-    -
_____   _____

4. Which two words start with **h**?

_____   _____
-    -
_____   _____

Name: _____

Spelling Week 11

☆ **Week 11 Rule:** Magic **e** can jump back only one letter to make a vowel long.

Rules We've Learned
- The letters **ch** say **/ch/** like in **chipmunk**.
- The letters **th** say **/th/** like in **thumb**.
- The letters **sh** say **/sh/** like in **shark**.
- Short **e** says **/e/** like in **hen**.
- The letters **ar** say **/ar/** like in **arm**.
- Short **o** says **/o/** like in **frog**.

ate	gate	cake	rake
made	whale	shape	tape
were	you	one	what
sight word	sight word	sight word	sight word

Sight words do not necessarily follow rules.

Name: _____

Word Search

Find and circle the spelling words. All words read horizontally and left to right. There may be additional words in the puzzle.

h	o	n	e	y	z	d	w	h	a	t	t
s	y	z	m	y	o	u	t	o	p	a	b
t	r	m	w	e	r	e	v	q	t	u	s
o	s	h	a	p	e	x	l	t	a	p	e
m	a	d	e	f	o	w	h	a	l	e	t
t	c	f	r	o	g	r	a	k	e	o	p
c	a	k	e	i	d	o	m	f	i	x	w
b	o	g	a	t	e	t	y	o	x	c	e
c	s	i	a	t	e	a	y	s	b	y	t

Spelling Words

ate

gate

cake

rake

made

whale

shape

tape

were

you

one

what

Draw a picture of the sentence in the box.

The fat whale ate the cake.

Unscramble the Sentence

Cut and paste the words onto the lines in the correct order to make a sentence. Use the capital and period as clues. Draw a picture of your sentence.

made	a	cake.	The	whale	you	big

Name: _____

Match the Picture

Name the picture. Circle the word for the picture. Then write the word on the line.

ate
gate
mate

_____

take
cake
shape

_____

rake
you
ship

_____

what
one
were

_____

Spelling Week 12

☆ **Week 12 Rules:** When a **c** is followed by an **e** or an **i**, it can make the sound **/s/** as in **sail**.

As **s** can sound like a **/z/** in **zipper** when it is between two vowels.

Rules We've Learned

- Magic **e** can jump back one letter to make a vowel long.
- The letters **ch** say **/ch/** like in **chipmunk**.

- The letters **th** say **/th/** like in **thumb**.
- The letters **sh** say **/sh/** like in **shark**.

ride	hide	nice	mice
nose	rose	drove	vote
no	like	yes	all
sight word	sight word	sight word	sight word

Sight words do not necessarily follow rules.

Name: _____

Sort the Vowels

Write the words under the same long vowel sound.

ride	nice	nose	drove
hide	mice	rose	vote

light

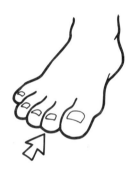

toes

_____

_____

_____

_____

_____

Name: _____

Fill in the Missing Word

ride	nice	nose	drove	no	yes
hide	mice	rose	vote	like	all

1. Will you go on a _____ with me.

2. A _____ smells nice.

3. She _____ the car.

4. Do you _____ me?

5. I like to _____ at the top.

6. We _____ sat on the rug.

Name: _____

Spelling Art

Draw a picture of each word. Copy the word neatly.

hide	**nose**	**mice**
rose	**ride**	**drove**

Name: _____

Spelling Week 13

☆ **Week 13 Rule:** An **s** can sound like a **/z/** when it is between two vowels.

Rules We've Learned
- Magic **e** can jump back only one letter to make a vowel long.
- The letters **ch** say **/ch/** like in **chipmunk**.
- The letters **sh** say **/sh/** like in **shark**.

use	fuse	cute	huge

sheep	street	meet	green

be	we	what	when
sight word	sight word	sight word	sight word

Sight words do not necessarily follow rules.

62   ©*Teacher Created Materials, Inc.*

Name: _____

Sort the Vowels

Write the words under the same long vowel sound.

use	cute	sheep	meet
fuse	huge	street	green

mule

eagle

_____

_ _ _ _ _ _ _ _ _ _ _ _ _ _ _ _

_____

_ _ _ _ _ _ _ _ _ _ _ _ _ _ _ _

_____

_ _ _ _ _ _ _ _ _ _ _ _ _ _ _ _

_____

Name: _____

Riddle Fun

Answer the riddle. Write the correct word on the line.

cute	huge	sheep	street	we	green

1. I'm a little chick. I'm _____ .

2. I'm white and fluffy. I'm a _____ .

3. I'm so big. I'm _____ .

4. You can cross me. I'm a _____ .

5. Me, be, and _____ all rhyme.

6. I'm a frog. I'm _____ .

Name: _____

Word Search

Find and circle the spelling words. All words read horizontally and left to right. There may be additional words in the puzzle.

h	o	c	u	t	e	d	w	a	t	t	e
s	f	u	s	e	a	o	h	u	g	e	y
t	r	u	s	e	r	s	h	e	e	p	s
o	w	h	a	t	e	x	w	h	e	n	l
m	a	s	t	r	e	e	t	h	a	l	e
t	c	m	e	e	t	r	a	k	e	o	p
l	c	g	r	e	e	n	o	m	b	e	x
w	w	e	g	a	t	e	t	y	o	x	p
c	w	h	e	n	t	e	a	b	y	t	o

Spelling Words

use

fuse

cute

huge

sheep

street

meet

green

be

we

what

when

Draw a picture of the sentence in the box.

The green sheep sat on the street.

Name: _____

Spelling Week 15

☆ **Week 14 Rule:** When there are two vowels together, "the first vowel does the talking and the second vowel does the walking." In other words, the first vowel says its name. For example, in the word **each**, the **e** says **/e/** and the **a** says nothing.

Rules We've Learned
- An **s** can sound like a **/z/** when it is between two vowels.
- Magic **e** can jump back only one letter to make a vowel long.
- Always use the letters **ck** after a short vowel to make the **/k/** sound.

Spelling Sentence: Look at these quick mice eat meat.

eat	**meat**	**each**	**scream**
squeal	**dream**	**quick**	**quit**
from	**these**	**you**	**your**
sight word	sight word	sight word	sight word

Sight words do not necessarily follow rules.

66

Name: _____

Word Search

Find and circle the spelling words. All words read horizontally and left to right.
There may be additional words in the puzzle.

e	a	t	x	y	o	u	r	m	z	a	t
x	y	z	m	e	a	t	v	w	s	t	l
t	m	s	q	u	e	a	l	q	m	p	e
x	t	v	q	d	r	e	a	m	y	o	u
c	h	c	s	c	r	e	a	m	e	q	u
c	k	q	u	i	t	x	q	u	i	c	k
m	f	t	h	e	s	e	a	f	l	x	w
f	r	o	m	n	e	t	o	e	a	c	h

Spelling Words

at

meat

each

scream

squeal

dream

quick

quit

from

these

you

your

Finish the sentence in the box. Then draw a picture.

I like to dream about _____.

Name: _____

Unscramble the Sentence

Cut and paste the words onto the lines in the correct order to make a sentence.
Use the capital and period as clues. Draw a picture of your sentence.

| Look | at | quick | mice | these | eat | meat. |

68

Name: _____

Rhyming Fun

Write a rhyming word from the list for each word below.

eat	each	squeal	quick	from	you
meat	scream	dream	quit	these	your

1. beach _____

2. sit _____

3. dream _____

4. beat _____

5. tick _____

6. seal _____

7. cheese _____

Write these words one time each.

from	**these**	**your**
_____	_____	_____

Spelling Week 16

☆ **Week 15 Rules:** A **y** can sound like a long **/e/** when it occurs at the
end of a word or syllable.
The letters **ay** together say long **/a/**.

Rules We've Learned

- When there are two vowels together, "the first vowel does the talking
  and the second vowel does the walking." In other words, the first
  vowel says its name. For example, in the word **each**, the **e** says **/e/** and
  the **a** says nothing.
- An **s** can sound like a **/z/** when it is between two vowels.

Spelling Sentence: The baby pony played in the rain with the lady.

lady	**baby**	**pony**	**rain**
mail	**pail**	**play**	**say**
once	**come**	**was**	**with**
sight word	sight word	sight word	sight word

Sight words do not necessarily follow rules.

Match the Picture

Name the picture. Circle the word for the picture. Then write the word on the line.

pine
pony _____
bony _____

baby
shady _____
bite _____

rake
rain _____
pain _____

make
mail _____
pail _____

Practice your spelling sentence on the back of this page.

Name: _____

Word Practice

Trace over each word and write it twice more.

lady

baby

pony

rain

mail

pail

play

say

Name: _____

Sentence Writing

Write each sight word in a sentence.

once	come	was	with

1.

2.

3.

4.

Spelling Week 1

☆ **Week 16 Rule:** The letters **igh** say long /i/, and a **y** in a short word with no vowels says long /i/.

Rules We've Learned
- A **y** on the end of a word says /e/.
- The letters **ay** together say long /a/.
- An **s** can sound like a /z/ when it is between two vowels.
- Magic **e** can jump back only one letter to make a vowel long.

Spelling Sentence: I try not to cry when it is dark at night.

right	night	sight	high
try	cry	dry	fly
why	they	this	by
sight word	sight word	sight word	sight word

Sight words do not necessarily follow rules.

Name: _____

Riddle Fun

Answer the riddle. Write the correct word on the line.

right	night	high	try	cry	fly	they

1. I play in the day. I sleep in the _____ .

2. I put my _____ hand over my heart
when I say the Pledge.

3. When I am sad, I _____ .

4. This word rhymes with **say**, but doesn't look the same. The word is
_____ .

5. I'm not down low. I'm up _____ .

Name: _____

Unscramble the Sentence

Cut and paste the words onto the lines in the correct order to make a sentence. Use the capital and period as clues. Draw a picture of your sentence.

high	I	night?	Can	at	fly	up

76

Name: _____

Sentence Writing

Write each sight word in a sentence.

why	they	this	by

1.

2.

3.

4.

Spelling Week 18

☆ **Week 17 Rule:** The letters **ow**, **oa**, **oe**, and an **o** by itself can say long **/o/**.

Rules We've Learned

- The letters **igh** say long **/i/**, and a **y** in a short word with no vowels says long **/i/**.

- A **y** on the end of a word says **/e/**.

- When two vowels are together, "the first vowel does the talking and the second vowel does the walking." In other words, the first vowel says its name. In the word **each**, the **e** says **/e/** and the **a** says nothing.

Spelling Sentence: Did you see the yellow snowman in the boat?

snowman	**yellow**	**grow**	**throw**
boat	**goat**	**float**	**cold**
gold	**toe**	**was** sight word	**saw** sight word

Sight words do not necessarily follow rules.

Name: _____

Sentence Writing

Write each sight word in a sentence.

was	saw

1.

2.

Trace over the spelling sentence.

Did you see the yellow snowman in the boat?

Name: _____

Word Search

Find and circle the spelling words. All words read horizontally and left to right. There may be additional words in the puzzle.

w	a	s	t	c	y	e	l	l	o	w	a
x	y	g	r	o	w	v	w	s	a	i	h
v	b	o	a	t	h	e	l	p	l	m	x
t	h	r	o	w	v	d	o	c	d	f	rd
u	c	k	l	x	o	g	o	a	t	m	j
f	l	o	a	t	s	n	o	w	m	a	n
c	o	l	d	d	k	c	g	o	l	d	t
t	s	a	w	m	t	o	e	h	e	l	p

Spelling Words

snowman

yellow

grow

throw

boat

goat

float

cold

gold

toe

was

saw

Draw a picture of the sentence in the box.

I saw a snowman in a yellow boat.

Name: _____

Spelling Art

Draw a picture of each word. Copy the word neatly.

snowman	goat	boat
_____	_____	_____
gold	toe	yellow
_____	_____	_____

Spelling Week 18

☆ **Week 18 Rules:**   The letters **ow** can also make the sound in **cow**.

The letters **ew** and **ue** can sound like a long **/u/**.

Rules We've Learned

- The letters **ow**, **oa**, **oe**, and an **o** by itself can all say long **/o/**.
- The letters **igh** say long **/i/**, and a **y** in a short word with no vowels says long **/i/**.
- A **y** on the end of a word says **/e/**.
- The letters **ch** say **/ch/** like in **chipmunk**.

Spelling Sentence: The fat brown cow went downtown to find a few flowers.

how	now	brown	cow
downtown	shower	flower	few
rescue	which	were	when
	sight word	sight word	sight word

Sight words do not necessarily follow rules.

Name: _____

Word Search

Find and circle the spelling words. All words read horizontally and left to right. There may be additional words in the puzzle.

how	brown	downtown	flower	rescue	were
now	cow	shower	few	which	when

w	i	l	l	o	w	t	f	e	w
h	e	t	n	o	w	k	k	l	l
r	e	s	c	u	e	j	k	l	w
o	p	h	o	w	j	j	n	l	k
d	o	w	n	t	o	w	n	w	n
a	d	n	t	c	o	w	e	h	e
s	h	o	w	e	r	n	e	m	e
n	t	w	h	f	l	o	w	e	r
t	b	r	o	w	n	t	t	t	j
l	w	h	i	c	h	h	o	w	p
c	o	w	h	e	n	w	e	r	e
a	n	d	w	h	e	n	t	x	h

Practice your spelling sentence on the back of this page.

Name: _____

Rhyming Fun

Write the spelling word on the line next to the word it rhymes with.

brown	downtown	flower	rescue	were
cow	shower	few	which	when

1. hen _____

2. flower _____

3. her _____

4. itch _____

5. chew _____

6. shower _____

7. how _____

8. down _____

Circle the words below that have the **/ow/** sound like in **cow**.

shower	few	were	brown	how

Name: _____

Word Practice

Trace over each word and write it twice more.

how

now

brown

cow

few

which

were

when

rescue

Spelling Week 19

☆ **Week 19 Rules:** The letters **ou** can make a sound like in **cow**.
The letters **au** and **aw** make the sound in **saw**.

Rules We've Learned
- The letters **ow** can also make the sound in **cow**.
- The letters **ew** and **ue** can sound like a long **/u/**.
- The letters **ow**, **oa**, **oe**, and an **o** by itself can all say long **/o/**.
- An **s** can sound like a **z** when it is between two vowels.
- Magic **e** can jump back only one letter to make a vowel long.

Spelling Sentence: Who saw the mouse in the house?

shout	house	mouse	about
saw	hawk	August	because
draw	paw	were sight word	who sight word

Sight words do not necessarily follow rules.

Name: _____

Word Search

Find and circle the spelling words. All words read horizontally and left to right. There may be additional words in the puzzle.

shout	about	August	paw
house	saw	because	were
mouse	hawk	draw	who

a	b	c	s	h	o	u	t	d	f	g	h	l	j	m	n
s	a	w	o	t	c	t	y	h	g	n	m	b	k	j	l
m	o	s	y	o	m	o	u	s	e	t	h	e	t	t	h
e	w	u	g	h	v	b	n	m	o	p	l	d	r	a	w
t	h	s	s	g	t	h	e	y	h	u	j	k	l	m	n
p	q	e	s	o	t	s	a	w	t	h	y	r	q	p	o
m	n	r	l	u	t	t	h	h	s	h	a	w	k	m	n
p	a	w	A	u	g	u	s	t	t	h	l	m	o	p	o
a	b	o	u	t	p	h	o	u	s	e	b	e	c	a	u
b	e	c	a	u	s	e	t	w	e	r	e	y	l	o	p
m	n	o	p	q	r	s	t	h	e	w	h	o	m	a	n
l	e	t	a	b	v	h	o	p	a	w	a	a	d	t	t
c	h	a	w	c	s	t	e	v	e	b	a	d	g	e	t

Practice your spelling sentence on the back of this page.

Name: _____

Rhyming Fun

Choose a spelling word to rhyme with the word and write it on the line.

shout	paw	hawk	draw
mouse	saw	August	were
house	about	because	who

1. boo _____

2. raw _____

3. claw _____

4. house _____

5. chalk _____

6. mouse _____

7. snout _____

8. stout _____

9. fur _____

10. thaw _____

Circle the words below that have the **/aw/** sound like in **hawk**.

because	about	were	saw	August

Name: _____

Word Practice

Trace over each word and write it twice more.

shout

mouse

about

paw

saw

August

were

who

because

Name: _____

Spelling Week 20

☆ **Week 20 Rule:** The letters **oo**, **ue**, and **ew** all make the sound in **hoot**.

Rules We've Learned

- **Au** and **aw** make the sound in **saw**.
- The letters **ow** can also make the sound in **cow**. The letters **ew** and **ue** can sound like a long **/u/**.
- The letters **ou** can make a sound like in **cow**.
- The letters **ow**, **oa**, **oe**, and an **o** by itself can all say long **/o/**.
- Magic **e** can jump back only one letter to make a vowel long.

Spelling Sentence: The spoon looks blue in the moonlight.

food	**cool**	**spoon**	**moonlight**
glue	**blue**	**true**	**rule**
grew	**new**	**with** sight word	**have** sight word

Sight words do not necessarily follow rules.

Name: _____

Picture Match

Name the picture. Circle the word for the picture. Then write the word on the line.

spin
soon
spoon

_____

fight
food
fin

_____

moonlight
midnight
daylight

_____

blue
true
glue

_____

new
cool
grew

_____

Name: _____

Rhyming Fun

Choose a spelling word to rhyme with the word and write it on the line.

food	spoon	glue	true	grew	with
cool	moonlight	blue	rule	new	have

1. fool _____

2. crew _____

3. due _____

4. rude _____

5. moon _____

Choose a word to write in a sentence. Remember to use capitals and periods.

with	have

_____

_____

_____

Name: _____

Word Search

Find and circle the spelling words. All words read horizontally and left to right.
There may be additional words in the puzzle.

food	spoon	glue	true	grew	with
cool	moonlight	blue	rule	new	have

a	b	c	s	f	o	o	d	f	g	h	l	w	i	t	h
s	a	w	o	t	c	t	y	c	o	o	l	b	k	j	l
m	o	s	y	o	m	o	u	s	e	t	h	e	t	t	h
s	p	o	o	n	v	b	g	r	e	w	l	d	r	a	w
g	l	u	e	g	t	h	e	y	h	a	v	e	l	m	n
o	p	q	e	m	o	o	n	l	i	g	h	t	r	q	p
l	m	n	r	l	u	t	t	h	h	s	h	a	w	k	m
p	a	w	a	u	g	u	s	t	t	h	l	m	o	p	o
a	b	o	u	t	p	h	o	u	s	e	b	e	c	a	u
b	e	c	a	u	s	e	t	w	e	r	e	y	l	o	p
m	n	o	p	q	r	s	t	h	e	w	h	r	u	l	e
n	e	w	a	b	b	l	u	e	a	w	a	a	d	t	t
c	h	a	w	k	s	t	t	r	u	e	a	d	g	e	t

Practice your spelling sentence on the back of this page.

Name: _____

Spelling Week 21

☆ **Week 21 Rule:** The letters **oo** can make the sound in **brook**.

Rules We've Learned
- A **k** before an **n** is silent, like in **know**.
- The letters **ow**, **oa**, **oe**, and an **o** by itself can all say long **/o/**.
- A **y** on the end of a word says **/e/**.
- The letters **ay** together says long **/a/**.

Spelling Sentence: He took the last good cookie.

look	**book**	**cookie**	**good**
stood	**took**	**know**	**knee**
knock	**put** sight word	**there** sight word	**where** sight word

Sight words do not necessarily follow rules.

Name: _____

Fill in the Missing Word

Fill in the blanks with a spelling word to complete the sentence.

knock	know	stood	cookie	book	there
knee	took	good	look	put	where

1. You read from a _____ .

2. The baby ate the _____ .

3. I have a very _____ dog.

4. Always _____ on the door.

5. "Ouch! My _____ hurts."

6. The boy _____ on a stool.

Name: _____

Word Practice

Trace over each word and write it twice more.

look

book

cookie

stood

there

where

know

knee

put

96

Name: _____

Rhyming Fun

Choose one of your spelling words to rhyme with the word and write it on the line. Each word may be used only once.

look	cookie	stood	know	knock	there
book	good	took	knee	put	where

1. hook _____

2. rookie _____

3. nook _____

4. lock _____

5. me _____

6. so _____

7. shook _____

8. would _____

9. foot _____

10. care _____

Circle the words below that have the **/oo/** sound like in **book**.

good	**stood**	**knee**	**cookie**	**August**

Practice your spelling sentence on the back of this page.

Name: _____

Spelling Week 22

☆ **Week 22 Rules:** The letters **oy** and **oi** make the sound in **coil**.

   The letters **oy** usually come at the end of a word or syllable.

Rules We've Learned

- The letters **oo** can make the sound in **brook**.
- The letters **oo**, **ue**, and **ew** all make the sound in **hoot**.
- The letters **ow**, **oa**, **oe**, and an **o** by itself can all say long **/o/**.

Spelling Sentence: I would like a coin to pay for my new toy.

boy	**enjoy**	**toy**	**coin**
join	**coil**	**spoil**	**could** sight word
would sight word	**should** sight word	**are** sight word	**my** sight word

Sight words do not necessarily follow rules.

Name: _____

Find the Missing Word

Choose one of your spelling words to complete the sentence.

boy	toy	join	spoil	would	are
enjoy	coin	coil	could	should	my

1. I can see a girl and a _____ outside.

2. The dogs _____ big.

3. A dime is a silver _____ .

4. Let's _____ and hold hands.

5. I _____ playing outside.

6. Put the _____ in the toy box.

7. If I _____ be any animal, I'd be a horse.

8. My mom likes to _____ me.

Name: _____

Picture Match

Name the picture. Circle the word for the picture. Then write the word on the line.

chin
coil
coin

_____
- - - - - - - - - - - - - - - - -
_____

joy
join
jump

_____
- - - - - - - - - - - - - - - - -
_____

boy
toy
spoil

_____
- - - - - - - - - - - - - - - - -
_____

boy
are
would

_____
- - - - - - - - - - - - - - - - -
_____

Name: _____

ABC Order

Write these words in ABC order.

enjoy	join	are	my
boy	spoil	could	would

Name: _____

Spelling Week 23

☆ **Week 23 Rules:** The letters **ph** sounds like the **f** in **fun**.

In words that start with **wr**, the **w** is silent.

Rules We've Learned

- The letters **oy** and **oi** make the sound in **coil**.
- The letters **oy** usually come at the end of a word or syllable.
- A **k** before an **n** is silent, like in **know**.
- The letters **ow**, **oa**, **oe**, and an **o** by itself can all say long **/o/**.

Spelling Sentence: She took a photo of the wrong elephant!

wrong	**write**	**wrap**	**wrinkle**
photo	**phone**	**graph**	**elephant**
three	**just**	**friend** sight word	**all** sight word

Sight words do not necessarily follow rules.

Name: _____

Word Search

Find and circle the spelling words. All words read horizontally and left to right. There may be additional words in the puzzle.

wrong	wrap	photo	phone	elephant	just
write	wrinkle	all	graph	three	friend

a	l	l	t	h	e	h	t	h	x	y	a	b	c	d	e	f	t
d	g	d	f	r	i	e	n	d	a	b	e	j	u	s	t	t	a
a	a	a	s	a	s	u	s	a	n	n	e	t	h	r	e	e	r
e	l	e	p	h	a	n	t	a	n	d	m	m	o	n	e	a	m
g	r	a	p	h	i	n	g	i	s	f	u	n	t	o	d	o	a
t	h	e	p	h	o	n	e	x	z	y	z	i	s	i	t	i	r
i	l	i	k	a	r	e	n	p	h	o	t	o	i	y	i	n	a
i	h	a	v	e	a	w	r	i	n	k	l	e	i	n	m	y	h
e	a	d	w	r	a	p	t	h	e	g	i	f	t	i	w	r	e
i	a	t	t	e	t	w	r	w	r	i	t	e	i	t	i	a
a	b	y	t	a	b	w	r	o	n	g	t	h	i	s	i	s	n

Practice your spelling sentence on the back of this page.

Name: _____

Spelling Practice

Trace over each word and write it twice more.

wrong

write

wrap

photo

phone

graph

elephant

three

just

wrinkle

Name: _____

Sentence Writing

Write each sight word in a sentence.

friend	all

1.

2.

Trace over the spelling sentence.

She took a photo of the

wrong elephant!

Name: _____

Spelling Week 24

☆ **Week 24 Rules:** Add the letters **ed** to make the past tense.

The letters **er** makes the sound like in **her**.

Rules We've Learned

- The letters **ph** sounds like the **f** in **fun**.
- In words that start with **wr**, the **w** is silent.

Spelling Sentence: The teacher asked us to do our homework.

asked	pulled	washed	planted
started	thunder	powder	carpenter
teacher	baker	our	here
		sight word	sight word

Sight words do not necessarily follow rules.

Name: _____

Story Writing

asked	planted	powder	baker
pulled	started	carpenter	our
washed	thunder	teacher	here

Use as many spelling words as you can to finish the story. There may be more than one choice. Be creative! Highlight your spelling words.

One fine spring day, a _____

_____

_____ **a seed.**

One day, the seed _____ **to**

grow. All of a sudden it started to rain and

_____

_____. **The**

_____

_____ **said, "Let's get out of**

_____

_____.

In the end, _____

_____

_____.

Name: _____

Sentence Writing

Choose four spelling words to write in a sentence.

asked	planted	powder	baker
pulled	started	carpenter	our
washed	thunder	teacher	here

1. _____

_____

2. _____

_____

3. _____

_____

4. _____

_____

Name: _____

Word Practice

Trace over each word and write it once more.

asked

pulled

washed

planted

started

thunder

powder

carpenter

teacher

baker

our

Name: _____

Spelling Week 25

☆ **Week 25 Rule:** The letters **ur**, **ir**, and **er** make the sound in **bird**.

Rules We've Learned
- Add the letters **ed** to make the past tense.
- The letters **er** makes the sound like in **bird**.

Spelling Sentence: The bird was sad to see the little girl hurt on her birthday.

church	**burst**	**hurt**	**turn**
bird	**first**	**third**	**birthday**
little	**thank**	**why** sight word	**they** sight word

Sight words do not necessarily follow rules.

Name: _____

Rhyming Fun

Find the spelling word that rhymes.

burst	turn	first	thank	they
hurt	bird	third	why	

1. cry _____

2. burn _____

3. third _____

4. tank _____

5. shirt _____

6. bird _____

7. first _____

8. thirst _____

9. way _____

 #3284 Building Blocks to Spelling

Name: _____

Word Practice

Trace over each word and write it once more.

church

burst

hurt

turn

bird

first

birthday

why

little

they

thank

Name: _____

Riddle Fun

Answer the riddle. Write the correct word on the line.

church	third	birthday	lay	thank	little

1. On Sunday, he goes to _____ .

2. She can't wait to celebrate her _____ .

3. I want to be first, second, or _____ .

4. An elephant is big and a mouse is _____ .

5. Remember to say "please" and " _____ you."

6. A chick can _____ an egg.

Name: _____

Spelling Week 26

☆ **Week 26 Rule:** The letters **dge** after a short vowel says **/j/** like in **jump**.

Rules We've Learned

- The letters **ur**, **ir**, and **er** make the sound in **bird**.
- Add the letters **ed** to make the past tense.
- In words that start with **wr**, the **w** is **silent**.

Spelling Sentence: The strong judge loves to eat fudge under the bridge.

bridge	fudge	pledge	hedge
badge	judge	shred	scrape
throw	splash	squeak	strong

114

Name: _____

Rhyming Fun

Find the spelling word that rhymes.

hedge	shred	throw	squeak	bridge
judge	scrape	splash	strong	

1. fudge _____

2. pledge _____

3. snow _____

4. long _____

5. bed _____

6. tape _____

7. flash _____

8. beak _____

9. ridge _____

JUDGE SMITH

Name: _____

Word Search

Find and circle the spelling words. All words read horizontally and left to right. There may be additional words in the puzzle.

bridge	**pledge**	**badge**	**shred**	**throw**	**squeak**
fudge	**hedge**	**judge**	**scrape**	**splash**	**strong**

```
a f b r i d g e r i t h i d s d h s h e d g e
w h e n i s a n t h e i f u d g e a i t h t h
p l e d g e i s a i w t h c m z b a d g e i l
s h r e d t i t h e s c r a p e h t h e l s a
s q u e a k i w h e r e h e i s t j u d g e l
t s p l a s h t h e i t h e t h r o w n t h e
i a m a i a m a n h s t r o n g t h a t h e u
s c r a p e r i f f r i e n d t h i t h r o w
```

Practice your spelling sentence on the back of this page.

Name: _____

Spelling Practice

bridge _____

fudge _____

pledge _____

shred _____

scrape _____

throw _____

splash _____

squeak _____

strong _____

hedge _____

badge _____

Name: _____

Spelling Week 27

☆ **Week 27 Rule:** The letter **i** by itself can make a long **/i/** like in **kind**.

Rules We've Learned

- The letters **dge** after a short vowel says **/j/** like in **jump**.
- The letters **ur**, **ir**, and **er** make the sound in **bird**.
- Add the letters **ed** to make the past tense.

Spelling Sentence: Please, can you help me find my first grade book?

find	kind	mind	behind

climb	after	how	again
	sight word	sight word	sight word

where	there	when	water
sight word	sight word	sight word	sight word

Sight words do not necessarily follow rules.

Name: _____

Spelling Practice

Trace over each word and write it twice more.

find _____

kind _____

mind _____

behind _____

water _____

climb _____

there _____

again _____

where _____

after _____

how _____

Name: _____

ABC Order

Write these words in ABC order.

find	mind	where	behind
kind	again	there	how

Name: _____

Sentence Writing

Write each sight word in a sentence.

where	there

1.

2.

Trace over the spelling sentence.

Please, can you help me

find my first grade book?

Spelling Week 28

☆ **Week 28 Rules:** The letters **alk** form a spelling pattern that makes the sound in **walk**.

The letters **all** form a spelling pattern that makes the sound in **call**.

Rules We've Learned

- The letter **i** by itself can make a long **/i/** like in **kind**.
- The letters **ur**, **ir**, and **er** make the sound in **bird**.
- Add the letters **ed** to make the past tense.

Spelling Sentence: I love to see the leaves in October.

walk	**talk**	**chalk**	**fall**
mall	**smaller**	**all**	**call**
tall	**September**	**October**	**does** *sight word*

Sight words do not necessarily follow rules.

Name: _____

Unscramble the Sentence

Cut and paste the words onto the line in the correct order to make a sentence.
Use the capital and period as clues. Draw a picture of your sentence.

like	I	to	the	walk	in	fall.

Name: _____

Spelling Practice

Trace over each word and write it once more.

walk

talk

chalk

fall

all

call

smaller

does

mall

September

October

Name: _____

Sentence Writing

Write each sight word in a sentence.

again	water

1.

2.

Trace over the spelling sentence.

I love to see the leaves

fall in October.

Name: _____

Spelling Week 29

☆ **Week 29 Rules:** The letters **ing** form a spelling pattern that makes the sound in **king**.
The letters **ly** make the sound as in **slowly**.

Rules We've Learned
- The letters **alk** form a spelling pattern that makes the sound in **walk**.
- The letters **all** form a spelling pattern that makes the sound in **call**.
- Add the letters **ed** to make the past tense.

Spelling Sentence: The king was running quickly when he saw a kite flying in the sky.

king	thing	running	jumping
flying	shouting	slowly	quickly
was	saw	when	your
sight word	sight word	sight word	sight word

Sight words do not necessarily follow rules.

Name: _____

Story Writing

king	jumping	slowly	saw
thing	flying	quickly	when
running	shouting	was	your

Use as many spelling words as you can to finish this story. There may be more than one choice. Be creative! Highlight your spelling words.

Once upon a time, there lived a

_____

_____ **who**

_____

_____

_____

_____

_____

_____

_____

_____

_____

_____

_____

_____

Name: _____

ABC Order

Write these words in ABC order.

king	running	flying	was
thing	jumping	shouting	your

128

Name: _____

Riddle Fun

Answer the riddle. Write the correct word on the line.

running	king	flying	saw	slowly	jumping

1. The _____ wore a shiny crown.

2. I watched a cheetah _____ very fast.

3. A lion runs quickly. A turtle walks _____.

4. I _____ a really funny show on TV.

5. My teacher always makes us do _____ jacks in the morning.

6. I am in an airplane. I am _____ .

Name: _____

Spelling Week 30

☆ **Week 30 Rules:** When the letter **g** is followed by **e** or **i**, it can make the sound **/j/** like in **jump**.

A **g** before an **n** is silent as in **gnat**.

Rules We've Learned

- The letters **ing** form a spelling pattern that makes the sound in **king**.
- The letters **alk** form a spelling pattern that makes the sound in **walk**.
- The letters **all** form a spelling pattern that makes the sound in **call**.
- The letter **i** by itself can make a long **/i/** like in **kind**.

Spelling Sentence: The gentle panda gnawed on a large stick.

gnaw	**gnash**	**gem**	**large**
gentle	**cage**	**giant**	**second**
want	**when**	**there**	**their**
sight word	sight word	sight word	sight word

Sight words do not necessarily follow rules.

Name: _____

Story Writing

gnaw	large	giant	when
gnash	gentle	second	there
gem	cage	want	their

Use as many spelling words as you can to finish this story. There may be more than one choice. Try to use describing words correctly in your story. Be creative! Highlight your spelling words.

Once upon a time, there lived a

_____

_____

_____

_____

_____ .

One day, _____

_____

_____

_____

_____

_____

_____

_____

_____ .

Name: _____

ABC Order

Write these words in ABC order.

large	cage	their
gentle	second	when

Practice your spelling sentence on the blank of this page.

Name: _____

Find the Missing Word

Choose one of your spelling words to complete the sentence.

gnaw	large	cage	want
gem	gentle	second	when

1. My dog likes to _____ on a bone.

2. I _____ to eat some cookies.

3. Huge, giant, and _____ all mean "big."

4. A ruby is a kind of _____ stone.

5. Next year, I will be in _____ grade.

6. Put the tiger in the _____ .

7. _____ is it time for lunch?

Circle the words with the **/j/** sound like in edge.

gnaw	gem	large	cage	gnash	giant

Spelling Week 31

☆ **Week 31 Rules:** The letter **y** can make the sound of long vowel **/e/** or **/i/** at the end of a word or syllable, like in the words **baby** and **cry**. Change **y** at the end of a word when it has the sound of long **/e/** or long **/i/** to **i** when adding an ending like **ed**, **er**, or **est**. To make a plural with a word that ends in **y** (when it has the sound of long **/e/** or long **/i/**), change the **y** to **i** and add **es**.

Spelling Sentence: The fat baby was funnier than all the rest of the babies.

happy	**happier**	**happiest**	**funny**
funnier	**funniest**	**city**	**cities**
baby	**babies**	**your**	**our**
		sight word	sight word

Sight words do not necessarily follow rules.

Name: _____

Fill in the Blanks

Fill in the blank with the correct spelling word.

happiest	happier	funniest	funny
city	babies	your	our

1. The boy is happy. I am _____ .

2. New York is the name of a big _____ .

3. The _____ like to drink milk.

4. The clown tells the _____ jokes at the circus.

5. Give me _____ money.

6. The winner of the game is the _____ person.

7. Bunny and _____ rhyme.

Name: _____

Sentence Writing

Write each sight word in a sentence.

your	happiest

1. _____

_____

2. _____

_____

Trace over the spelling sentence.

The fat baby was funnier

than all the rest of the

babies.

Name: _____

Spelling Practice

happy

happier

happiest

funny

funnier

funniest

city

cities

baby

babies

your

Name: _____

Spelling Week 32

☆ **Week 32 Rule:** The letters **le** make the **/l/** sound at the end of a word.

Rules We've Learned

- The letters **ing** form a spelling pattern that makes the sound in **king**.
- The letters **ge** and **gi** both make the sound **/j/** like in **jump**.

Spelling Sentence: There was a very large fiddle sitting on the brown table.

table	**candle**	**fable**	**fiddle**

one	**two**	**four**	**eight**
sight word	sight word	sight word	sight word

give	**some**	**very**	**lived**
sight word	sight word	sight word	sight word

Sight words do not necessarily follow rules.

Name: _____

Word Search

Find and circle the spelling words. All words read horizontally and left to right. There may be additional words in the puzzle.

table	fable	one	four	give	very
candle	fiddle	two	eight	some	lived

a	b	l	i	v	e	d	x	f	g	h	l	j	w	i	t	h
s	a	w	o	t	a	b	l	e	x	o	o	l	b	k	j	l
m	o	v	e	r	y	o	u	s	e	t	h	e	t	t	h	s
p	o	o	n	c	a	n	d	l	e	w	l	d	r	a	w	z
g	l	s	o	m	e	h	e	f	i	d	d	l	e	m	n	o
o	p	f	g	i	v	e	o	f	a	b	l	e	t	r	q	p
o	l	m	n	l	u	t	t	h	h	s	h	a	w	k	m	n
n	p	a	w	a	u	g	u	l	m	o	n	e	x	y	x	m
b	e	c	a	u	s	e	t	w	o	r	e	y	l	o	p	l
m	n	o	f	o	u	r	h	e	w	h	r	u	l	e	p	r
n	e	k	a	r	e	n	u	a	n	d	a	a	d	t	t	k
v	e	r	y	k	s	u	s	a	n	e	i	g	h	t	t	o

Name: _____

Spelling Fun

table	fable	one	four	give	very
candle	fiddle	two	eight	some	lived

1. On the back of this paper, write each word one time.

2. Write four words that end with the sound **/l/.**

_____   _____

_____   _____

_____   _____

3. Write a word that rhymes with **bun**.

_____

_____

4. Which four words are number words?

_____   _____

_____   _____

_____   _____

140   ©Teacher Created Materials, Inc.

Name: _____

Story Writing

table	fiddle	four	some
candle	one	eight	very
fable	two	give	lived

Use at least four spelling words to finish this story. Be creative! Highlight your spelling words.

Once upon a time, there _____

_____

_____

_____

who wanted _____

_____

_____

_____ .

One day, _____

_____

_____

_____

_____

_____

_____ .

Answer Key

Week 1

Spelling Fun
1. Write each word one time on back.
2. pat, hat, at
3. am, ham
4. tap, to

Unscramble the Sentence
The hat is on the ham.

Word Search
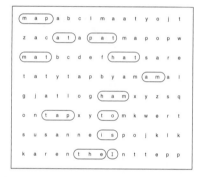

Week 2

Word Search
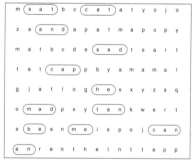

Word Fun
1. Write each word one time on back of page.
2. an or can
   cat or sat
   cap or tap
3. sat, be, sad

Unscramble the Sentence
He sat on the sad cat.

Week 3

Sort the Vowels
cat: and, hand, sand, as
pig: sit, hip, did, pin

Word Search
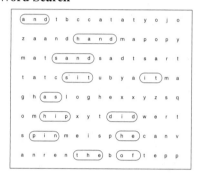

Unscramble the Sentence
He can sit in the sand.

Week 4

Unscramble the Sentence
The big fat pig can dig fast.

Sort the Vowels
1. pig, big, dig, if, fin
2. fat, fan, fast

Fill in the Missing Word
1. dig   3. pig   5. see
2. fin   4. big, fat

Week 5

Word Search
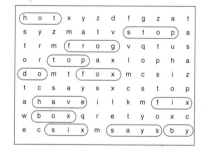

Fill in the Missing Word
1. stop   3. hot   5. box
2. frog   4. top   6. have

Sort the Vowels
stop, frog, box, fox six, fix

Week 6

Spelling Art
Check to see if the drawing matches the word.

Unscramble the Sentence
Are you too far from the star?

Sort the Sounds
1. car, bar, barn, far, star, arm, farm, hard, are
2. you, my, was

Week 7

Spelling Art
Check to see if the drawing matches the word.

Rhyming Fun
1. up, cup; rug, bug; run, fun
2. be, lip

Fill in the Missing Word
1. me   3. do   5. this
2. run   4. with   6. bug

Week 8

Word Search
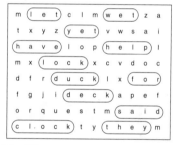

Spelling Fun
2. wet, let, yet
3. lock, clock
4. duck, deck

Unscramble the Sentence
They have a wet duck.

Week 9

Riddle Fun
1. thin   3. that   5. shark
2. wish   4. fish   6. shop

Unscramble the Sentence
What is that thin fish for?

Sort the Sounds
1. this, that, thin, with
2. shop, shark, wish, fish
3. when, what
4. are

Week 10

Match the Picture
chin, lunch, chick, math, shell

Answer Key

Unscramble the Sentence
The chick is still in her shell.

Spelling Fun
1. Write each word one time on the back of the page.
2. chin, chick, chip
3. shell, she
4. her, his

Week 11
Word Search

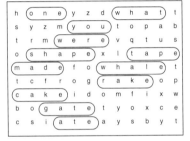

Unscramble the Sentence
The whale made you a big cake. or The big whale made you a cake.

Match the Picture
gate, cake, rake, one

Week 12
Sort the Vowels
light: nice, mice, hide, ride
toes: drove, vote, nose, rose

Fill in the Missing Word
1. ride
2. rose
3. drove
4. like
5. hide
6. all

Spelling Art
Make sure the picture matches the word.

Week 13
Sort the Vowels
mule: fuse, huge, cute, use
eagle: meet, green, street, sheep

Riddle Fun
1. cute
2. sheep
3. huge
4. street
5. wet
6. green

Word Search

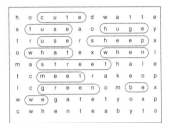

Week 14
Word Search

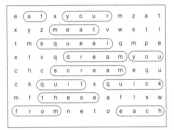

Unscramble the Sentence
Look at these quick mice eat meat.

Rhyming Fun
1. each
2. quit
3. scream
4. meat
5. quick
6. squeal
7. these

Week 15
Match the Picture
pony, baby, rain, pail

Week 16
Riddle Fun
1. night
2. right
3. cry
4. they
5. high

Unscramble the Sentence
Can I fly up high at night?

Week 17
Word Search

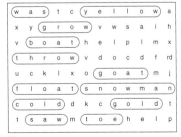

Spelling Art
Check to see if the drawing matches the word.

Week 18
Word Search

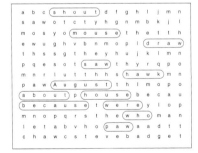

Rhyming Fun
1. when
2. shower
3. were
4. which
5. few
6. flower
7. now or cow
8. brown
9. how, now, or cow
10. how, now, or cow

Week 19
Word Search

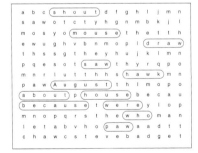

Rhyming Fun
1. who
2. paw, saw, or draw
3. paw, saw, or draw
4. mouse
5. hawk
6. house
7. shout or about
8. shout or about
9. were
10. paw, saw, or draw
Circle: saw, August

Answer Key

Week 20
Match the Picture
spoon, food, moonlight, glue, grew
Rhyming Fun
1. cool or rule
2. true, blue, glue, grew, or new
3. true, blue, glue, grew, or new
4. food
5. spoon
Word Search

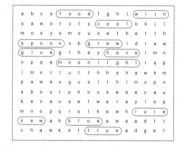

Week 21
Fill in the Missing Word
1. book   3. good   5. knee
2. cookie 4. knock 6. stood
Rhyming Fun
1. look, book, or took
2. cookie
3. look, book, or took
4. knock
5. knee
6. know
7. look, book, or took
8. stood or good
9. put
10. there or where
Circle: good, stood, cookie

Week 22
Find the Missing Word
1. boy   4. join   7. could
2. are   5. enjoy 8. spoil
3. coin 6. toy
Match the Picture
coin, join, toy, boy
ABC Order
are, boy, could, enjoy, join, my, spoil, would

Week 23
Word Search

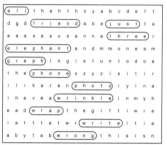

Sort the Sounds
1. wrong, wrap, write, wrinkle
2. phone, graph, elephant, photo
3. all

Week 25
Rhyming Fun
1. why   4. thank   7. burst
2. turn   5. hurt   8. first
3. bird   6. third   9. they
Riddle Fun
1. church   3. third   5. thank
2. birthday 4. little 6. lay

Week 26
Rhyming Fun
1. judge   4. strong   7. splash
2. hedge   5. shred   8. squeak
3. throw   6. scrape   9. bridge
Word Search

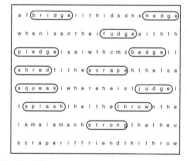

Week 27
ABC Order
again, behind, find, how, kind, mind, there, where

Week 28
Unscramble the Sentence
I like to walk in the fall.

Week 29
ABC Order
flying, jumping, king, running, shouting, thing, was, your
Riddle Fun
1. king
2. running
3. slowly
4. saw
5. jumping
6. flying

Week 30
ABC Order
cage, gentle, large, second, their, when
Find the Missing Word
1. gnaw   4. gem   6. cage
2. want   5. second 7. When
3. large
Circle: gem, large, cage, giant

Week 31
Fill in the Blanks
1. happier
2. city
3. babies
4. funniest
5. your
6. happiest
7. funny

Week 32
Word Search

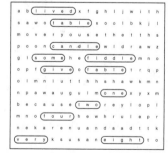

Spelling Fun
1. Write each word one time on back.
2. fiddle, table, candle, fable
3. one
4. one, two, four, eight